Living IN THE
Presence OF God

Titles in the *Thirty Days with a Great Spiritual Teacher* series:

ALL WILL BE WELL
Based on the Classic Spirituality of *Julian of Norwich*

GOD AWAITS YOU
Based on the Classic Spirituality of *Meister Eckhart*

LET NOTHING DISTURB YOU
A Journey to the Center of the Soul with *Teresa of Avila*

PEACE OF HEART
Based on the Life and Teachings of *Francis of Assisi*

TRUE SERENITY
Based on Thomas á Kempis' *The Imitation of Christ*

SIMPLY SURRENDER
Based on the Little Way of *Thérèse of Lisieux*

WHERE ONLY LOVE CAN GO
A Journey of the Soul into *The Cloud of Unknowing*

YOU SHALL NOT WANT
A Spiritual Journey Based on *The Psalms*

LET THERE BE LIGHT
Based on the Visionary Spirituality of *Hildegard of Bingen*

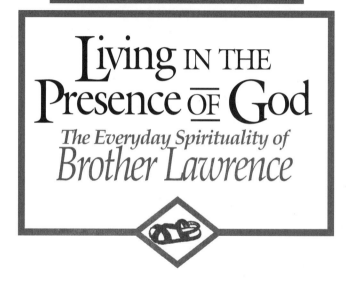

30 Days with a Great Spiritual Teacher

Living IN THE Presence OF God

The Everyday Spirituality of
Brother Lawrence

AVE MARIA PRESS Notre Dame, Indiana 46556

John Kirvan is the editor and author of several books, including *The Restless Believers*, and currently lives in southern California where he writes primarily about classical spirituality.

The passages from *The Practice of the Presence of God* are a modern translation and paraphrase developed for meditational use from the early English editions. They incorporate passages from the basic text, his letters, maxims, and contemporary biographical material.

© 1997 Quest Associates.
International Standard Book Number: 0-87793-601-3
Cover and text design by Elizabeth J. French.
Printed and bound in the United States of America.

Kirvan, John J.
        Living in the presence of God : the everyday spirituality of Brother Lawrence / John Kirvan.
            p.   c.m. — (30 days with a great spiritual teacher)
        ISBN 0-87793-601-3
        1. Devotional Calendars.   I. Lawrence, of the Resurrection, Brother, 1611–1691. Pratique de la présence de Dieu. English. Selections.   II. Title.   III. Series.
BV4811.K48   1997
242′ .2—dc21   96-39879
                                                                                        CIP

Contents

Brother Lawrence ◆ 7

How to Pray This Book ◆ 19

Thirty Days with Brother Lawrence ◆ 29

One Final Word ◆ 211

If I were a preacher
I would, above all other things,
preach the practice of the presence of God.
For there is nothing in the world
sweeter or more delightful
than a continual conversation with God.
I would advise the whole world to take it up,
so necessary do I consider it,
and so easy.

—Brother Lawrence

Brother Lawrence
of the Resurrection

There is something deeply encouraging and reassuring about a spirituality born in the steamy air of a kitchen and honed at a shoemaker's bench. It carries no trace of a hothouse world of spiritual luxury, exotic experience and leisure for the soul. It blossoms in a world where time is itself a luxury and the only space is where you find yourself.

Surely this is why so many who must pursue their soul's dreams and feed its hungers amid unremitting demands on their time, their energy, and their heart have for three centuries welcomed the wisdom of Brother Lawrence.

The book that became world famous as *The Practice of the*

Presence of God could just as easily have been called *The Prayer Life of a Working Man.* The man who would enter western literature and spiritual history as Brother Lawrence was born Nicolas Herman in 1614 in the village of Herimenil, near Luneville in Lorraine. Until his entry twenty-six years later into the order of Discalced Carmelites as a lay brother, we know very little about him. We know that he fought in the Thirty Years War and was wounded and captured. Then he was charged with being a spy, although the charge was dropped. Back in civilian life we know that he tried solitude for a while, a form of religious life for which he decided he was not suited. Subsequently, he spent some time as a gentleman's valet. Only then did he enter religious life, and even then at the lowest possible rung of monastic existence.

He began by reading all the right spiritual books, but each, he said, sent him off in a different direction, confusing his search for God rather than aiding it. So out of sheer need—and deep insight—he reduced his spiritual life to setting out to love God above all else, nurturing that love by consciously staying in God's presence, thinking about God as often as possible, and praying all the while he fulfilled the pedestrian but life-supporting duties of a cook and sandal-maker. Because of his status and his duties, he was not a regular or even frequent participant in the great quiet hours of prayer that were the lifeblood of the monks. The kitchen brothers prayed as their duties allowed.

As he sought to practice the presence of God in the midst of a busy life, he came to distrust, on the one hand, exotic religious experiences, and on the other, the distraction of dozens of little religious practices and devotions. How, he wondered, could we be content with so little, when God offers so much—himself?

His central insight was that to be open to such an offer we must avoid the two great temptations: "the other" and "the great." We are often tempted to believe that if only we were some *other* person, at some *other* time, in some *other* place, all would be well. Or if only our lives were not so tied to little things, and we had the opportunity for *great* deeds, we could be saints. But holiness, Brother Lawrence insists, does not depend on doing *other* things, or doing *great* things but simply in doing all the normal things of our daily life for the love of God. Our lives, no matter how inconsequential are not just the context of our pursuit, they are the stuff of spirituality. We live and grow on "staples."

12

Another insight was just as important. He talked often of resignation. For long stretches of his life he worked at a job for which he had no special attraction. Even worse, for a period of several years, he was convinced, despite his prayers, that he would be damned. There was even talk of dismissing him from the monastery. His response was consistent and profound: God will do what is best for me.

Living this way is not as easy as it sounds or as easy as Lawrence frequently promised. We need to learn what Lawrence learned only through years of spiritual pain. For although he had all the great tools for spiritual growth that a monastery and a great spiritual tradition could offer him, and although he lived consciously and continuously in the rewarding presence of God, he nevertheless lived for years believing that everything was against him, not just the standard enemies like "the world" and "the flesh" but reason, and God himself.

He was thrown back on naked faith, as indeed in the end we all will be.

"It doesn't matter," he concluded, "what I suffer or what I do provided that I remain lovingly united to his will."

"I am in the hands of God and he will do with me what he pleases."

"I began to live in perfect liberty and continual joy. I will die knowing that whatever becomes of me I have always done all that I did for the love of him."

The spirituality of Brother Lawrence is not, for all its accessible simplicity, superficial or shallow. It is in the deepest tradition of Western Christian spirituality, balancing the constant presence of God with the need for faith that can penetrate to the core of our world and our experience, and to the heart of God. It is about prayer, and most fundamentally the prayer of a working person, rooted and shaped by the necessities of a working day.

There is, Brother Lawrence assures us, no great art or science to living in the presence of God, to praying as he did. "Thoughts count for little. Love does everything."

In over three centuries there have been hundreds of editions in many languages of the work generally called *The Practice of the Presence of God*. It is not a book conceived and written by Lawrence, but a compilation of various materials. As a result, one edition can vary quite greatly from another in its contents. Generally speaking, you will find the sixteen letters from Lawrence to persons seeking his spiritual advice. There is also a gathering of maxims in which Lawrence sums up in his own words the basics of a spiritual life lived in the presence of God. You may also find a eulogy composed in the year following his death by someone who had great access to Lawrence while he was alive. There are transcripts of conversations and a summary of his "ways." You will find all these components skillfully translated, and placed in historical context in the critical edition recently published by ICS Publications. Nothing currently available compares to it.

The thirty meditations in this book are designed to provide a concentrated, meditative exposure to the principle ideas that characterized the life and teachings of Brother Lawrence. Any one meditation may bring together passages from several sources and each has been composed in the first person so that Lawrence is presented as speaking directly to you, a seeker after his hard won wisdom. I hope that the experience offered in this book will not only be a rewarding spiritual journey for you, but that you will be prompted to read—and pray—the whole of *The Practice of the Presence of God.*

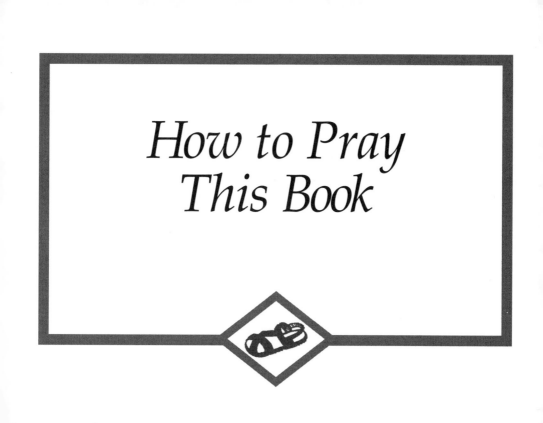

*How to Pray
This Book*

The purpose of this book is to open a gate for you, to make accessible the spiritual experience and wisdom of one of history's most attractive spiritual teachers, Brother Lawrence. *The Practice of the Presence of God* is a great spiritual document that has, for three centuries, conveyed important and basic spiritual insights.

This is not a book for mere reading. It invites you to meditate and pray its words on a daily basis over a period of thirty days.

It is a handbook for a spiritual journey.

Before you read the "rules" for taking this spiritual journey, remember that this book is meant to free your spirit, not confine it. If on any day the meditation does not resonate well for you, turn elsewhere to find a passage which seems to best fit the spirit of your day and your soul. Don't hesitate to repeat a day as often as you like until you feel that you have discovered what the Spirit, through the words of the author, has to say to your spirit.

Here are suggestions on one way to use this book as a cornerstone of your prayers.

As Your Day Begins

As the day begins set aside a quiet moment in a quiet place to read the meditation suggested for the day

The passage is short. It never runs more than a couple of hundred words, but it has been carefully selected to give a spiritual focus, a spiritual center to your whole day. It is designed to remind you as another day begins of your own existence at a spiritual level. It is meant to put you in the presence of the spiritual master who is your companion and teacher on this journey. But most of all the purpose of the passage is to remind you that at this moment and at every moment during this day you will be living and acting in the presence of a God who invites you continually, but quietly, to live in and through him.

A word of advice: read slowly. Very slowly. The meditation has been broken down into sense lines to help you do just this. Don't read just to get to the end, but to savor each part of the meditation. You never know what short phrase, what word, will trigger a response in your spirit. Give the words a chance. After all, you are not just reading this passage, you are praying it. You are establishing a mood of serenity for your whole day. What's the rush?

All Through Your Day

Immediately following the day's reading you will find a

sentence or phrase which we call a mantra, a word borrowed from the Hindu tradition. In this book it is usually borrowed from the day's reading. It is designed to be a companion for your spirit as you move through a busy day. Write it down on a 3" x 5" card or on the appropriate page of your daybook. Look at it as often as you can. Repeat it quietly to yourself and go on your way.

It is not meant to stop you in your tracks or to distract you from responsibilities, but simply, gently, to remind you of the presence of God and your desire to respond to this presence.

There are many ways to use a mantra. Simply repeating to yourself the word or phrase is the most obvious and most widely used. In this particular journey with Brother Lawrence, you may wish to select a single, evocative word from the suggested phrase. Use it by itself or combine it in your mind and prayer with its opposite. For example, on one day the suggested mantra contains the word "joy." Match it up in your prayers with "sorrow" and see where the spirit leads you.

As Your Day Is Ending

This is a time for letting go of the day.

Find a quiet place and calm your spirit. Breath deeply. Inhale, exhale—slowly and deliberately, again and again until you feel your body let go of its tension.

Now read the evening prayer slowly, phrase by phrase. You may recognize at once that we have taken one of the most familiar evening prayers of the Christian tradition and woven into it phrases taken from the meditation with which you began your day and the mantra that has accompanied you all through your day. In this way, a simple evening prayer gathers together the spiritual character of the day that is now ending as it began—in the presence of God.

It is a time for summary and closure.

Invite God to embrace you with love and to protect you through the night.

Sleep well.

Some Other Ways to Use This Book

1. Use it any way your spirit suggests. As mentioned earlier, skip a passage that doesn't resonate for you on a given day, or repeat for a second day or even several days a passage whose richness speaks to you. The truths of a spiritual life are not absorbed in a day, or for that matter, in a lifetime. So take your time. Be patient with the Lord. Be patient with yourself.

2. Take two passages and/or their mantras—the more contrasting the better—and "bang" them together. Spend time discovering how their similarities or differences illumine your path.

3. Start a spiritual journal to record and deepen your experience of this thirty-day journey. Using either the mantra or another phrase from the reading that appeals to you, write a spiritual account of your day, a spiritual reflection. Create your own meditation.

4. Join millions who are seeking to deepen their spiritual life by joining with others to form a small group. More and more people are doing just this to support each other in their mutual quest. Meet once a week or at least every other week to discuss and pray about one of the meditations. There are many books and guides available to help you make such a group effective.

Thirty Days with
Brother Lawrence

Day One

◆◆◆◆◆

My Day Begins

Early on in your spiritual efforts,
you may discover as I did
that every book you read
will lay out a different route for reaching God.
They may be more confusing than helpful,
doing little to show you
how to become God's alone.

So choose instead, as I have,

to give all for all to God
with the hope that he will take away your sins.
For love of him,
renounce every thing that is not him,
and begin to live simply
as if there were no one in the world
except him and you.

All Through the Day

All of me.

My Day Is Ending

Stay with me Lord
as another day
spent in your presence
fades into darkness
and silence.

Help me
to pull myself together
out of the thousand strains
of an ordinary day
into one simple act of love for you.
There are, I know,
a thousand roads to your love,
for those who are wiser and holier

than I can imagine.
I need a simple path.

Forgive my sins.
Accept all that I am,
all that I could be,
that in return
I might have nothing but you,
only you,
all of you.

Day Two

◆◆◆◆◆

My Day Begins

Without the continuous help of God
we cannot escape the dangers
that abound in this life.
So how can you expect his continuous help
unless you pray for it continually?

But how can you pray to him continually
unless you are in his presence?

And how can you be in his presence
unless you think of him often?

And how can you think of him often
unless you develop
the habit of living in his presence?

All Through the Day

God is a habit of the heart.

My Day Is Ending

Stay with me Lord
as another day living in your presence
fades into darkness
and silence.

Stay with me
to help me through this night
and all the nights to come.
And through all the days
remind me of your presence,
so that I can go on praying

and thinking about you,
hour by hour,
until living aware of you becomes
the deepest habit of my heart.

Day Three

◆◆◆◆◆

My Day Begins

The more you come to know God,
the more you will desire to know him.
And since knowledge is commonly
the measure of love,
the deeper and more extensive
your knowledge becomes,
the greater will be your love.

The worst thing that can happen

is that you may lose your sense of God.
But trust in his goodness;
he will never completely forsake you.
Rather, he will give you the strength
to bear whatever difficulties
come your way.
And never be afraid.

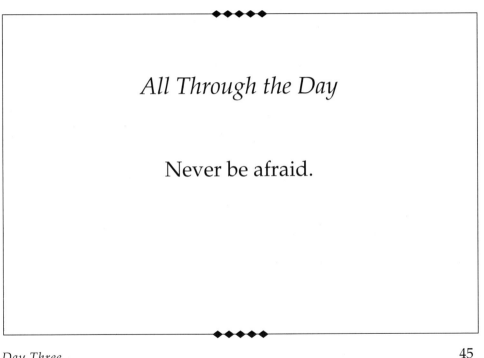

All Through the Day

Never be afraid.

My Day Is Ending

Stay with me Lord
as another day living in your presence
fades into darkness
and silence.

Do not abandon me
to the nameless fears of the night
and what tomorrow may bring.
Replace the cowardice
of my heart
with trust in your love
and the strength

which help me bear
whatever difficulties
may come my way.

Let me not be afraid.

Day Four

◆◆◆◆◆

My Day Begins

Walk with God
in simple faith,
with humility and with love,
and try diligently
to do nothing and think nothing
that would displease him.

Make it your goal to persevere
simply and solely in his presence,
maintaining

habitual,
silent,
and secret
conversation of your soul with God.

And trust that when you have done
all you can do,
he will do
what is best for you.

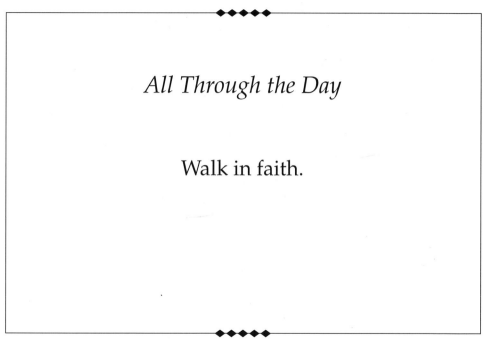

All Through the Day

Walk in faith.

My Day Is Ending

Stay with me Lord
as another day living in your presence
fades into darkness
and silence.

Do not let our quiet conversation
end here at the edge of night.
Let us speak with each other
in silence
and secrecy.
All through this day
I have sought
your presence,

doing whatever I could do for love of you.
Hear my quiet prayer now
and do, I ask of you,
whatever is best for me.

Day Five

◆◆◆◆◆

My Day Begins

There is no great art or science
to living in the presence of God.
You need only a heart
determined to apply itself
to no one or no thing but God.

Many of us fail to make progress
because we mistake

a multitude of penances
or a regimen of devotions
for the only thing that is important,
the love of God.

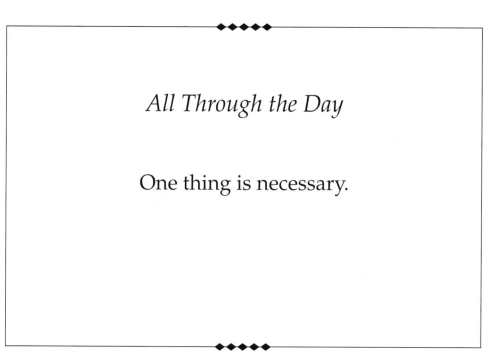

All Through the Day

One thing is necessary.

My Day Is Ending

Stay with me Lord
as another day living in your presence
fades into darkness
and silence.

Grant me a heart
determined to seek out
no one or nothing but you.
Clear my soul of
the thousand things

I mistake for you
and your love,
the only things
that are important.

Day Six

◆◆◆◆◆

My Day Begins

The key to living in the presence of God
is putting behind you everything
that you realize is not leading to him.
Only then will you become aware of
his presence within you.
Only then can you enter freely and simply
into a continual conversation with him,
asking his help,

seeking his will when you are in doubt,
doing well what he wants of you.

In every case,
aware of his presence,
dedicate your deeds to him
before you do them
and give thanks to him when you are done.

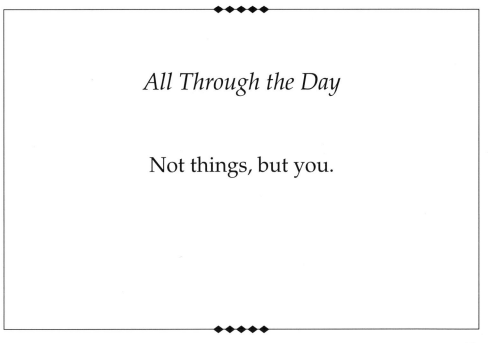

All Through the Day

Not things, but you.

My Day Is Ending

Stay with me Lord
as another day living in your presence
fades into darkness
and silence.

Increase my awareness
of your presence
so that I can enter
freely and simply

LIVING IN THE PRESENCE OF GOD

into a continual conversation with you
asking your help,
seeking your will,
doing well what you want of me.

Day Seven

◆◆◆◆◆

My Day Begins

I have tried from the beginning
to stay conscious of the presence of God,
not just at times of prayer,
but at every moment of every day,
even when I have been busiest with my tasks.
It has been painful and filled with difficulties.
My mind wanders.
So will yours.
But do not allow yourself

to become upset and worried.
Rather go on working
to keep out of your mind
anything and everything
that might interrupt
your sense of his presence,
your thoughts of him.

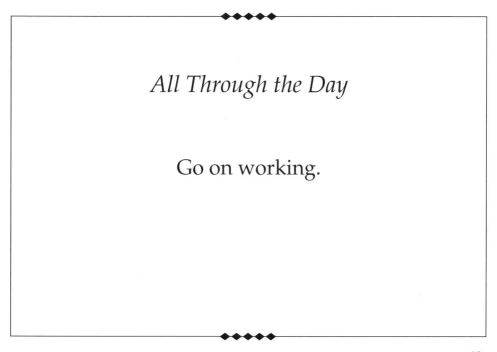

All Through the Day

Go on working.

My Day Is Ending

Stay with me Lord
as another day living in your presence
fades into darkness
and silence.

Even now,
here in the stillness of the night,
tell me that
I need not become upset and worried,
but rather, simply go on working
to keep out of my mind,
always,

anything and everything
that might interrupt
my sense of your presence,
my thoughts of you.

Day Eight

◆◆◆◆◆

My Day Begins

Staying with God
at the very center of your soul
may require you
to deprive yourself occasionally of innocent pleasures,
so that you can be entirely devoted to him.
But it does not mean doing violence to yourself.

No, you must serve God in holy freedom
without upset or disquiet,

recalling God to your mind,
mildly and tranquilly,
as often as you find it
wandering from him.

All Through the Day

In freedom and tranquillity.

My Day Is Ending

Stay with me Lord
as another day living in your presence
fades into darkness
and silence.

Teach me
to serve you
in holy freedom
without upset or disquiet,
recalling you
throughout the day

with mildness
and tranquillity,
and remembering you
in the silence of the gathering night.

Day Nine

◆◆◆◆◆

My Day Begins

There are great advantages
to practicing the presence of God.
When you are faithful to it
and set him always before your eyes,
you are far less likely to offend him.

But more importantly,
it will engender in you a holy freedom,
and if I may presume to say it,

a familiarity with God,
through which you will be
moved with confidence
to seek the graces you most need.

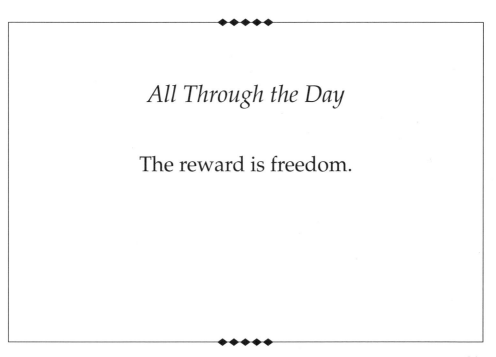

All Through the Day

The reward is freedom.

My Day Is Ending

Stay with me Lord
as another day living in your presence
fades into darkness
and silence.

Stay before my eyes.
Nourish in my spirit
that holy freedom
that you alone can give,
so that I might always

be at home in your presence,
and pray
with confidence
for the graces I most need.

Day Ten

◆◆◆◆◆

My Day Begins

From time to time
as you walk in the presence of God,
come before him
as the most wretched of people,
as someone who has committed
all sorts of crimes against him.
Confess your wickedness,
ask his forgiveness,
and abandon yourself into his hands

so that he might do with you as he pleases.

You will be surprised.
Rather than chastise you,
the Lord will embrace you with love,
seat you at his table, serve you with his own hands,
give you a key to his treasures,
and treat you as his favorite.

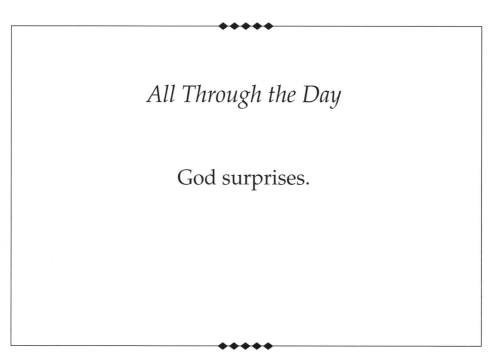

All Through the Day

God surprises.

My Day Is Ending

Stay with me Lord
as another day living in your presence
fades into darkness
and silence.

Let me not forget
how often
I have fled your presence.
Even as I remember my sins,
surprise me Lord
rather than chastise me.
Dare I ask
that you embrace me with your love,

seat me at your table,
serve me with your own hands,
give me a key to your treasures.
and treat me as your favorite?

Wrap me tightly
in your mercy.

Day Eleven

◆◆◆◆◆

My Day Begins

When I began my prayer life,
I followed the methods of the great teachers,
meditating on death and judgment,
on heaven and hell.
But for the rest of the day,
even when I was taken up with my kitchen tasks,
I applied my mind carefully
to the presence of God.
I thought of him as being not only with me

but within me.
Eventually I did the same thing
during my times of prayer.
It is this
that produced in me,
as it can in you,
a sense of God
that only faith can satisfy.

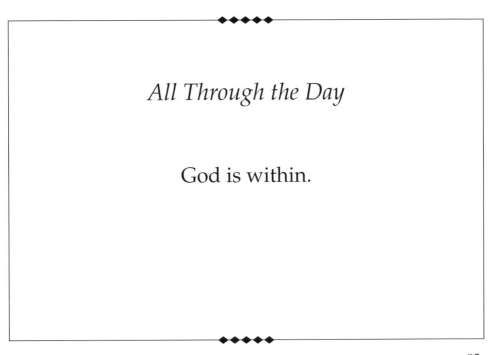

All Through the Day

God is within.

My Day Is Ending

Stay with me Lord
as another day living in your presence
fades into darkness
and silence.

You are not
"out there . . . somewhere . . ."
a vague presence in the universe
somewhere beyond the night sky,
but within me.
Let me not forget ever that.
Whether caught up
in the duties of my day

or in quiet times of prayer
such as this,
nourish me
with a sense of your presence
that only faith can see.

Day Twelve

◆◆◆◆◆

My Day Begins

Prayer is nothing else
but being aware of the presence of God.
It does not end
when the appointed times for "prayer" have passed.
For we pray whenever we do our ordinary tasks,
not with a view of pleasing others,
but as far as we are capable,
in order to please God.

You are called

to awareness of God's presence
always,
in times of activity,
as well as in the times
you set aside for prayer.

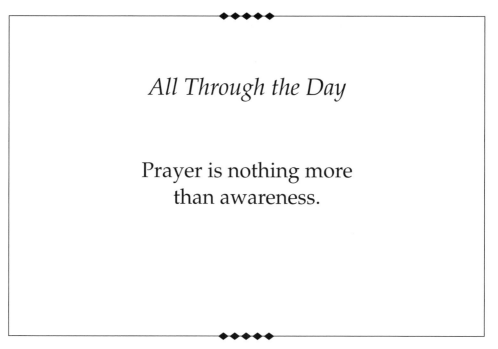

All Through the Day

Prayer is nothing more
than awareness.

My Day Is Ending

Stay with me Lord,
and let me go on praying,
as another day living in your presence
fades into darkness
and silence.

For if prayer is nothing else
but being aware of your presence,
it does not need to end
when the appointed times for "prayer"
have passed,
or even when the duties of the day
have ended.

For we pray whenever we
do what pleases you.
Accept then, I ask you,
my time of rest.
Hear the prayer
of this silent night.

Day Thirteen

◆◆◆◆◆

My Day Begins

When you pray,
don't multiply your words.
Many words and long speeches
are an excuse for your mind to wander.
Instead, present yourself to God
like a speechless beggar
at a rich man's gate.
Your only task is
to stay in the presence of God.

But when you pray,
if your mind does wander from God,
do not get upset.
Trouble and disquiet
are more likely to distract your soul
than bring it back to prayer.
Tranquillity is the key.
Just persevere
and God will have pity on you.

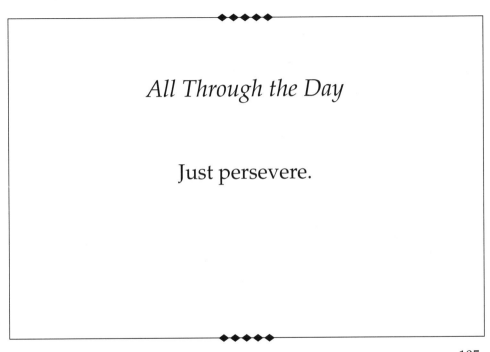

All Through the Day

Just persevere.

My Day Is Ending

Stay with me Lord
as another day living in your presence
fades into darkness
and silence.

Now is not the time
to search for words,
or to conjure up great thoughts,
but for silence.
I am a speechless beggar
at a rich man's gate.
My only task is

to stay in your presence.
Hear, I beg you,
what I cannot say,
what I need not say.

Day Fourteen

◆◆◆◆◆

My Day Begins

Speak to God in utter simplicity,
asking frankly and plainly for his help.
Say to him:
"I can't do anything without your help.
It is you alone
who can prevent me from falling,
and you alone
who can pick me up
when I do stumble."

I can tell you from experience
that God will never fail
to grant you the strength you need.
But you must ask.

LIVING IN THE PRESENCE OF GOD

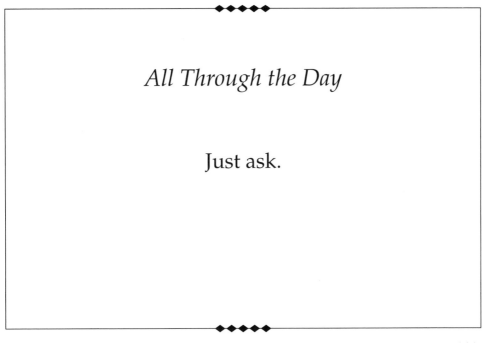

All Through the Day

Just ask.

My Day Is Ending

Stay with me Lord
as another day living in your presence
fades into darkness
and silence.

I can't do anything without your help,
not even enter this night with peace.
It is you alone
who can prevent me from falling
and you alone
who can pick me up
when I stumble.
It is you alone

who can quiet the confusion of this day,
and bring a silent, peaceful night
to my soul.
This I ask.

Day Fifteen

◆◆◆◆◆

My Day Begins

All the fine speeches I hear about God,
everything I have read about him,
all that I have come to feel about him,
have never been enough to satisfy me.
For being infinite in his perfection,
he is consequently beyond comprehension.
There are no words eloquent enough
to provide a perfect conception of his grandeur.

It is faith that reveals him

and lets us know him as he is.
Through faith
you will learn more about him in a short time
than you would in many years in the schools.

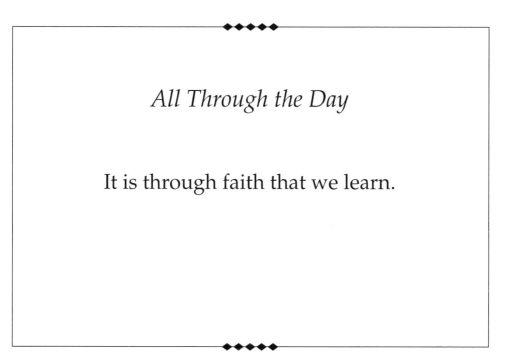

All Through the Day

It is through faith that we learn.

My Day Is Ending

Stay with me Lord
as another day living in your presence
fades into darkness
and silence.

I have no words eloquent enough
to capture you.
There are none.
Only faith can reveal you to me,
and allow me know you as you are.

So, my Lord
do not expect fine speeches

that will cut through my incomprehension,
but only silent faith
that is as wordless
as the quiet
of this dark night.

Day Sixteen

◆◆◆◆◆

My Day Begins

He alone can make himself known
as he really is.
But we go on searching
in philosophy and in science,
preferring, it seems, a poor copy
to the original
that God himself paints in the depths of our soul.

We bypass him there.
disdaining conversation with our King,

who is always present within us.
We prefer what books
tell us of him—
some comforting devotion
or a passing inspiration.

All Through the Day

He is as he is within us.

My Day Is Ending

Stay with me Lord
as another day living in your presence
fades into darkness
and silence.

It is tempting
to fill up these final minutes of the day
with the passing comforts
of easy devotions,
familiar words
that avoid you as you are.
Rather, let me

look to the face
you have painted
in the depths of my soul.
Let me silently
enjoy your presence
within me.

Day Seventeen

My Day Begins

God's treasury of gifts is unlimited.
Why settle for almost nothing?
Why be content with a little sensible devotion,
a passing warm feeling
that comes and goes in a minute?
Why blind yourself
to his riches,
hindering his generosity,
stemming the full flow of his love?

Your God
is infinitely gracious.
He knows what you need.
Hope in him.
Thank him for his generosity.
Take your comfort in him.

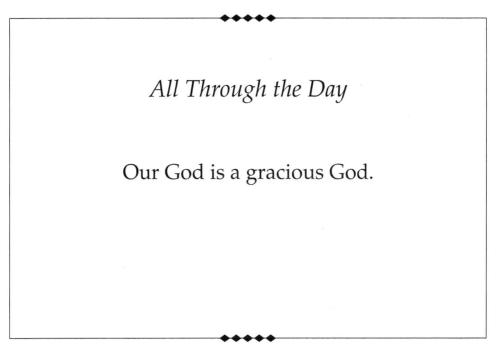

All Through the Day

Our God is a gracious God.

My Day Is Ending

Stay with me Lord
as another day living in your presence
fades into darkness
and silence.

Have I again settled for too little,
for almost nothing?
Your treasury of gifts is unlimited.
So why am I content
with passing warm feelings
that come and go in a minute?

Open my eyes to your riches.
Let me get out of the way
of your generosity.
Let me stop obstructing
the full flow of your love.

Day Eighteen

◆◆◆◆◆

My Day Begins

The way I recommend to you
is the way of faith.
You need always to quicken and enliven it,
for by itself,
it is enough to bring you
to a high degree of perfection.

In practice most of us have too little faith.
Instead of taking faith

as the standard of our spiritual life,
we amuse ourselves
with trivial devotions
that can, and often do,
change daily.

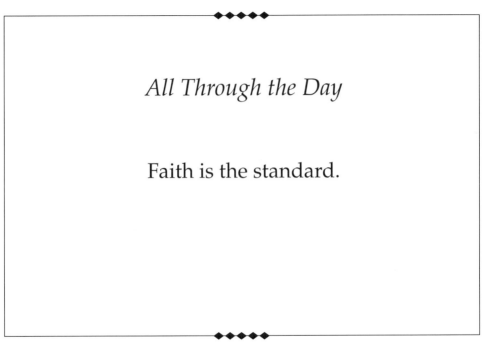

All Through the Day

Faith is the standard.

My Day Is Ending

Stay with me Lord
as another day living in your presence
fades into darkness
and silence.

There alone I can find you,
where only faith
is strong enough to go.
It is too easy
to stop this side of faith,
too inviting
to amuse myself

with trivial devotions
that can, and often do,
change daily.
There is no substitute for faith
on the journey
of my soul.

Day Nineteen

◆◆◆◆◆

My Day Begins

While it is true
that the foundation of a spiritual life is faith
nourished by thoughts of God,
you might sometimes go for quite a while
without thinking of God.
I do.
But it doesn't upset me.
Simply acknowledge your weakness before him
and return to him

with an even greater trust,
a trust that deeply honors him
and draws down
his greatest graces.

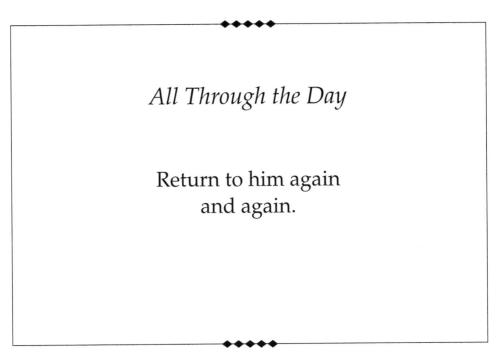

All Through the Day

Return to him again
and again.

My Day Is Ending

Stay with me Lord
as another day living in your presence
fades into darkness
and silence,
another day of hours passed
with hardly a thought of you.

But here in the gathering darkness
I admit my weakness before you
and return my heart and mind and soul to you

with an even greater trust.
Bestow, I ask of you,
on this forgetful seeker
your richest gifts.

Day Twenty

◆◆◆◆◆

My Day Begins

Whether God leads you
by suffering or consolation
will make no difference
if you truly resign yourself to finding his will.
But you can be sure
that there will be times of spiritual dryness,
of spiritual insensibility,
of exasperating difficulties
whenever you try to pray.

God will test your fidelity to him.
This is the time
to make good and effective
acts of resignation to his will,
for even one such act
could lead to spiritual growth.

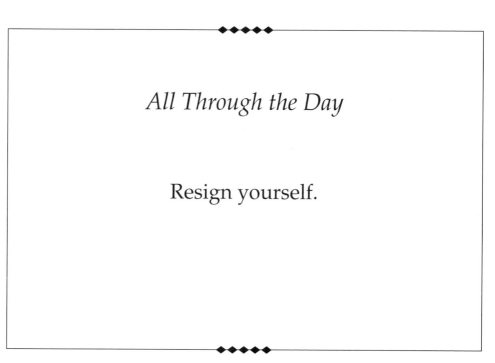

All Through the Day

Resign yourself.

My Day Is Ending

Stay with me Lord
as another day living in your presence
fades into darkness
and silence.

There were moments this day
when you seemed close enough to touch,
and other moments
when you have never seemed farther away,
moments that tested
all my quick and easy claims

of fidelity and love.
Now is the time
to resign myself
to your will.

Day Twenty-One

◆◆◆◆◆

My Day Begins

Once, for four long years,
I lived believing I was damned.
No one could persuade me differently.

But once I realized
that my problem was a lack of faith,
I began to live
in perfect liberty and continual joy.
Despite my sinfulness
God continued to bestow his blessings on me.

After all,
I entered upon the spiritual path
for no other reason
than the love of God,
and I have tried always
to act only for him.
So whatever becomes of me
I will die knowing
that I have always done
all that I could
out of love for him.

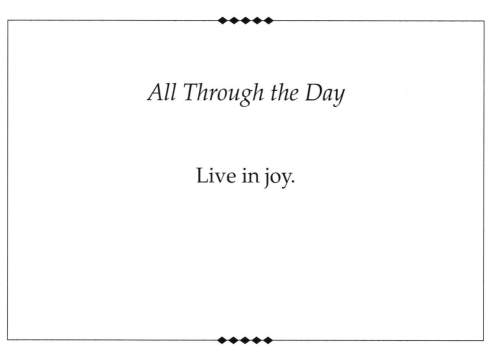

All Through the Day

Live in joy.

My Day Is Ending

Stay with me Lord
as another day living in your presence
fades into darkness
and silence
and take with it
my fear of losing you.

More than anything else,
I pray at the end of this day
for the perfect liberty
and continual joy
that only faith can bring.
For despite my sinfulness

you will, I know and trust,
continue to bestow
your blessings on me.
Help my unbelief.
Replace my fear with joy.

Day Twenty-Two

My Day Begins

Try always to be governed by love
and not by selfishness,
making the love of God
the goal of everything you do.

Even if it is only
to pick up a straw from the ground,
do it for the love of God,
seeking him only,

nothing else,
not even his gifts.

You will never find reason
to regret this way of living.

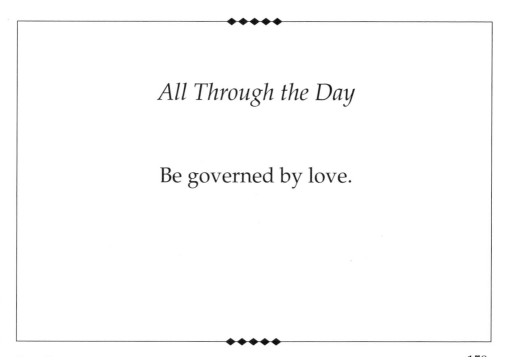

All Through the Day

Be governed by love.

My Day Is Ending

Stay with me Lord
as another day living in your presence
fades into darkness
and silence.

This was not a great day
filled with great deeds
and heroic love
but I did my best
with all the straws
I found in my path.
I picked them up
for the love of you,
seeking you only,

nothing else,
not even your gifts.

Love does
what love can do.

Day Twenty-Three

◆◆◆◆◆

My Day Begins

You can turn to God
with absolute confidence,
bringing to him
all your failures and sorrows.
Your God is infinitely generous.
But remember, he gives his gifts
in his own time
and when you least expect them.
Place all your hope in him, therefore,

thanking him for all his favors,
particularly for the fortitude and courage
with which he blesses you
in bad times.

All Through the Day

God acts in his own way,
in his own time.

My Day Is Ending

Stay with me Lord
as another day living in your presence
fades into darkness
and silence.

Let your infinite graciousness
fill the night,
hearing my prayers before they are said,
knowing what I want and need
before I know myself.
But let me be patient,

knowing that you give your gifts
in your own time
and when we least expect them.
All my hope is in you.

Day Twenty-Four

◆◆◆◆◆

My Day Begins

When God finds a soul
awash with a living faith
he pours into it the fullness of his graces.
There they flow like a torrent,
spreading themselves
wherever there is an opening.

But it is possible
to stand in the way of this flood of grace.
Let us do this no longer.

Let us make way for grace.
And let us not lose any time.
For we know not
how much time is left to us.

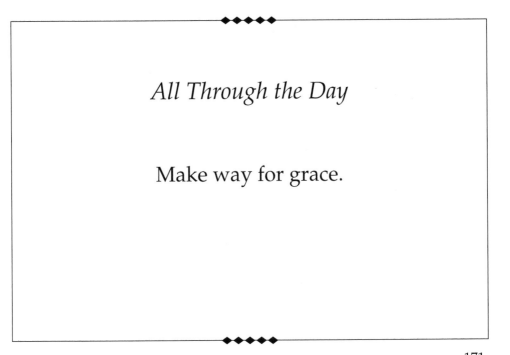

All Through the Day

Make way for grace.

My Day Is Ending

Stay with me Lord
as another day living in your presence
fades into darkness
and silence.

Pour the fullness of your graces
into my soul.
Let them flow like a torrent,
spreading themselves
wherever there is an opening.

I'm weary of
standing in the way of your grace.

Let me make way for you,
let me make room for you
in all the days that are left to me,
but especially
here in the silence of this night.

Day Twenty-Five

My Day Begins

I spent fifteen years working in the kitchen,
a job for which, I admit,
I had a natural aversion.
I had to pray all the time
for the grace to do God's work.
Only then did I find it easy.

Now I have a job I like.
But I could leave here
just as easily as I left the kitchen.

For in whatever place I find myself,
I can always do little things,
indeed all things,
for the love of God.
So can you.

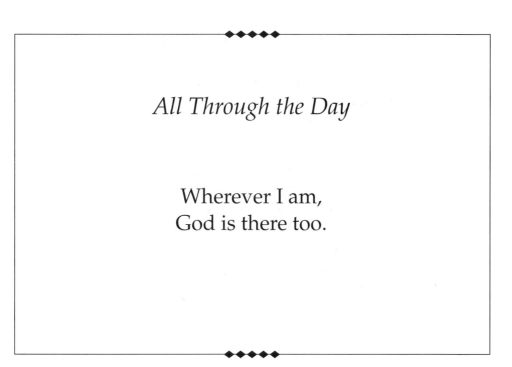

All Through the Day

Wherever I am,
God is there too.

My Day Is Ending

Stay with me Lord
as another day living in your presence
fades into darkness
and silence.

I entrust to you
all the small disappointments
and the passing joys of the day,
even my hopes for tomorrow.
It doesn't really matter where I am,
or with whom I am,
or what it is that I am called upon to do.

I need not be someone else;
I need not be some other place.
For in whatever place I find myself
I can always do little things,
indeed all things,
for the love of you.

Day Twenty-Six

My Day Begins

Your holiness does not depend
on doing "other" things,
but in doing for God's sake
what you would otherwise
normally do for your own sake.

You need not become weary
of doing little things
if you do them for the love of God.

Nor does it depend on your doing "great" things.

God is not concerned
with the greatness of your deeds,
but the love with which they are done.

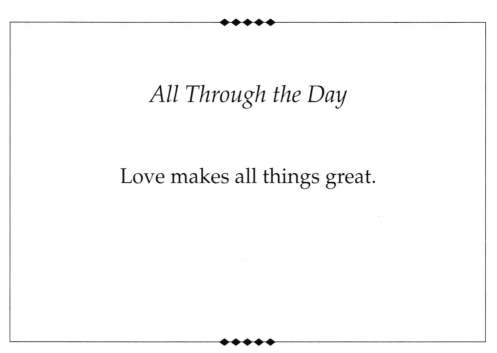

All Through the Day

Love makes all things great.

My Day Is Ending

Stay with me Lord
as another day living in your presence
fades into darkness
and silence.

Thank you for not making
a dream of holiness depend
on doing "other" things,
than what I must,
nor on doing "great" things.
Holiness requires only
that I do for your sake

the terribly ordinary things
that are the stuff of my life.

For I trust
that you are not concerned
with the greatness of my life,
but the love with which
I wish to live it.

Day Twenty-Seven

My Day Begins

It doesn't matter
what you do
or what you suffer,
provided that you remain
lovingly united to his will.

At one time,
there was talk of dismissing me
from the monastery.
I did not let it upset me,

for I knew
that I was and am
in the hands of God.
He will do with me—
with you—
what he pleases.
So if you cannot serve him
where you are,
you will serve him
where he wants you to be.

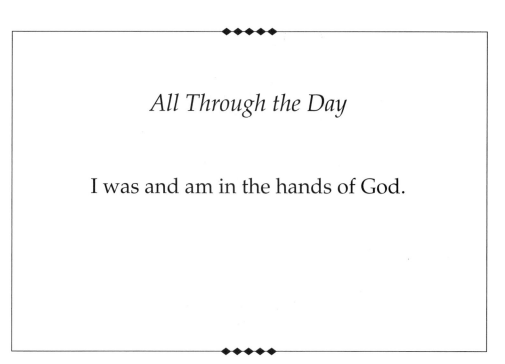

All Through the Day

I was and am in the hands of God.

My Day Is Ending

Stay with me Lord
as another day living in your presence
fades into darkness
and silence.

This day leaves behind it
reminders
that we do not
do your planning for you.
I know
that I was,
and am,
and always will be
in your hands.

LIVING IN THE PRESENCE OF GOD

You will do with me
what you please.
So if I cannot serve you
where I wish to be,
let me serve you
where you want me to be.

It doesn't matter
as long as I remain
lovingly united to your will.

Day Twenty-Eight

My Day Begins

In the ways of God,
thoughts count for little;
love does everything.

Therefore the shortest and most direct route
to God is to do everything
for the love of God,
and to use all the labors of your life
to demonstrate that love.

Maintain his presence within you
by this communion of your heart with his.
There is no mystery about this.
One only has to do it
generously and simply.

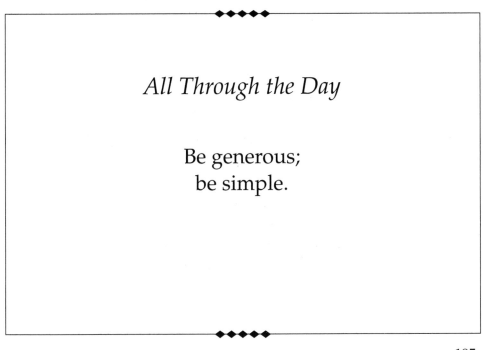

All Through the Day

Be generous;
be simple.

My Day Is Ending

Stay with me Lord
as another day living in your presence
fades into darkness
and silence.

Take my hand,
take my heart,
and lead me gently
into your world
where thoughts count for little,
and love does everything.

Let my own heart and hands.
echo the generosity of your love.

Carry me along
the shortest route to your heart.

Day Twenty-Nine

◆◆◆◆◆

My Day Begins

I know that to some,
maybe even to you,
my practice of the presence of God
seems to be
inactivity, delusion, and self-love.
I confess that it is a holy inactivity.
It might be self-love
if someone so aware of God's presence
were capable of it.

But I cannot bear to hear it called delusion,
because the soul who enjoys God in this way
desires nothing but him.

If I am deluded,
it is God's place to remedy it.
Let God do what he pleases with me.

I desire only him,
and to be wholly devoted to him.

LIVING IN THE PRESENCE OF GOD

All Through the Day

Do with me what you please.

My Day Is Ending

Stay with me Lord
as another day living in your presence
fades into darkness
and silence.

I desire to desire
nothing but you.
I know of no other way
to tell you of my desire,
to live out my desire,
than by paying,
as best I can,

LIVING IN THE PRESENCE OF GOD

simple attention to your presence.
If I am wrong,
if something else is needed,
I pray you,
remedy the failure of my heart.

Do with it what you please.

Day Thirty

———◆◆◆◆◆———

My Day Begins

If you turn inward
and faithfully practice the presence of God
it is possible
that your soul will become so intimate with God
that you will find yourself
spending practically all your time
in one continual act of prayer.

But understand that very few persons
reach this perfect state.

The rest of us can at least acquire,
with the help of ordinary grace,
a life lived
in the presence of God
wherever we are.

All Through the Day

Even I can live in the presence of God.

My Day Is Ending

Stay with me Lord
as another day living in your presence
fades into darkness
and silence.

Ignore the limitations
I place on your mercy.
Surprise me again
with your love,
your inexhaustible forgiveness,
your unquestioning welcome,
your generosity.

I have started out
on the path of living in your presence.
Let me not lose my way,
nor the sight of you.

One Final Word

Towards the end of his life, looking back over decades of single minded attention to the presence of God, Brother Lawrence confessed to being surprised:

> I came to the monastery these many years ago
> thinking that I would pay
> for my awkwardness and faults
> by sacrificing to God
> my life and all its pleasures.
> But God has disappointed me.
> I have met with nothing
> but satisfaction.

You can expect the same.

God always surprises, never disappoints, whatever spiritual path you take, whether it is that lived and recommended by Brother Lawrence or by some other great spiritual teacher.

If you decide that the path of Brother Lawrence is one that you wish to follow more closely and deeply, read and study the entire text of *The Practice of the Presence of God*, one that contains his letters, his maxims and other supplementary material.

You may, however, decide that his experience has not helped you. There are many other teachers. Somewhere there is the right teacher for your own, very special, absolutely unique journey of the spirit. You *will* find your teacher; you *will* discover your path.

We would not be searching, as St. Augustine reminds us, if we had not already been found.